8/12

Served with a flourish

Served with a flourish

Simon Lycett

LAUREL
GLEN

For Alexei, my beautiful godson, whose interest in food is already immense, and to Katey, Ruari, and Kirsty, who give such joy and are credits to their respective parents.

Published in North America by
Laurel Glen Publishing
5880 Oberlin Drive, Suite 400
San Diego, CA 92121-4794

ISBN 1-57145-646-5
Library of Congress Cataloging-in-Publication data available upon request.

A BERRY BOOK
Conceived, edited and designed by *Susan Berry* for Collins & Brown Limited.
Editor *Amanda Lebentz*
Designer *Debbie Mole*
Home Economist *Carole Handslip*

North American Edition
Publisher *Allen Orso*
Managing Editor *JoAnn Padgett*
Associate Editor *Elizabeth McNulty*

Reproduction by Classic Scan, pte Ltd, Singapore
Produced by Phoenix Offset, HK
Printed and bound in Cnina

CAUTION
Publisher's note: candles are included in several decorative ideas within this book. However, when lit, they are a fire hazard and must be treated with caution at all times. Never leave burning candles unattended.

CONTENTS

Introduction

A S A FLORAL decorator and party stylist, I am in the privileged position of being able to observe some of Britain's finest cooks, chefs, and caterers as I go about my daily business. I am also passionate about food and have a hearty appetite myself. I love to cook—it is my form of relaxation.

However, I am aware that for many people, food is nothing but a rather irritating necessity and for these individuals, the thought of organizing the daily feeding of the family is quite off-putting enough, while the very thought of preparing a dinner party or supper, even on the smallest of scales, would count as a nightmare of the most horrendous order.

Often, the root of this so-called aversion to cooking is a lack of confidence. Once people convince themselves that they don't have any culinary ability, they tend to stop trying. But I truly believe that it is quite possible, given a little guidance and with a few basic skills and store-bought ingredients, for everyone and anyone to serve perfectly acceptable, wholesome, appetizing food that not only tastes good but looks appealing too.

The phrase "beauty is in the eye of the beholder" is a truism that can also be applied to food and drink. The manner in which food is presented is, in my opinion, as important as the way it tastes, for no matter how delicious a dish may be, if it is unappealing to the eye it may never pass the lips. And by the same token, no matter how fancy and elaborate the presentation of a meal, if it has no taste to it, or worse still, if it tastes unpleasant, then nothing is gained.

The object of this book is therefore to encourage you to see beyond the obvious and the mundane preparation and decoration of foods, and to realize the enormous potential for making an enjoyable experience even better, with relatively little or even next-to-no effort at all. I am not merely concerned with celebratory meals or dishes for special occasions, but am suggesting the revision and upgrading of the everyday food we serve to our family, our partners, and our friends.

Even if you have invited someone to supper and warned them in advance that it will only be a very simple, unelaborate meal, there is absolutely no excuse for not paying attention to the finer details—all that is required is a little imagination, and as soon as you get into the habit of using it, applying your creativity in the kitchen will become second nature. Once you begin to experiment, your reputation as a great cook and entertainer will grow and flourish, no matter that most of what you serve is actually sold by a selection of well-known grocers and supermarkets!

In this book, I aim to show how even basic everyday meals such as soups, starters, and salads, can be transformed into delightful and appetizing culinary experiences. From simple ideas on presenting sauces, breads, vegetables, and butter, to imaginative ways in which to set the table and present food with a theme or in a more traditional style, I have delved into my own experiences and observations to come up with novel suggestions.

The setting of the table can have an enormous impact on the way in which food is perceived. Attractive, interesting, or unexpected combinations of linen, cutlery, crockery, and glassware make a definite statement and will effectively set the scene for the meal that is to follow. Give guests the impression that you care about these details and they will feel that you have made a real effort on their behalf—you really don't have to serve the most expensive ingredients to win their appreciation.

Take party canapés as an example: by proffering them in neat rows in a minimalist, contemporary style, they will look far more appealing than if piled awkwardly on a doily-covered plate. Swap standard cocktail sticks for longer more flamboyant bamboo skewers next time you serve finger food, and you will be amazed at the difference they make. Look again at the way you serve your favorite tried-and-true recipe: by preparing individual portions instead of a large dish, or experimenting with an unusual garnish, you could give a familiar meal a whole new lease on life …

Garnishes workshop

B E IT A twist of lemon peel placed discreetly on a steamed fillet of fish or a single edible flower perched atop a spring salad of mixed garden leaves, an interesting garnish can transform an ordinary dish into something extra-special. By mastering a few, very simple techniques you will be able to add a personal and novel flourish to every meal you serve.

Equipment

THE MAJORITY of utensils used to create the decorative effects featured in this book are readily available from everyday kitchen equipment stores. You will probably have most of the equipment already, even if you do not tend to use it too often! There are a few, more specialized tools, such as a parmesan knife or nutmeg grater, that may prove helpful, although in many cases, you will probably be able to improvize (with an ordinary knife or a fine cheese grater, for example) if you do not have a specific piece of equipment at hand.

If you should decide to invest in some specialized tools and equipment, simply refer to the lists provided on this page, and overleaf, where you will find all the tools you could possibly need to recreate the ideas given later in the book. Before you make your purchase, remember that you get what you pay for, so it's best to decide how much use you are going to get from a particular implement and how long you want it to last before spending a fortune on something that is simply going to sit in a kitchen drawer! Expensive, top-of-the-line knives are often a good investment since they are manufactured from the finest steel and will last almost a lifetime, even when used on a daily basis. However, it probably won't be worth your while to spend a similar amount on a canelli knife that you may only pick up very occasionally.

A few of the tools featured are so specific that you may like to share the expense with a cooking friend by each buying one or two of them and then pooling your tools when required. But it really isn't necessary to possess every tool listed: decide first how useful each piece of equipment will be. For example, few people need three different types of palette knife, and if you know that you're never going to become a real icing enthusiast, it is pointless splurging on all the specialized icing tools!

1 Zester, for removing wider strips of lemon zest.

2 Small zester, for removing thin strips of lemon zest.

3 Hand-held grater for grating parmesan cheese or chocolate.

4 Sharp kitchen scissors, an essential for all sorts of jobs.

5 Nutmeg grater, also useful for grating other small items.

6 Cook's knife.

7 Potato peeler.

8 Grapefruit knife.

9 Serrated cheese knife, with pronged tip.

10 Icing tongs, for crimping.

11 Parmesan cheese knife, good for cutting tough rind.

12 Skewer, keep several of these handy for all sorts of jobs.

13 Icing tool, for shaping fondant or making fondant flowers. Tapered palette

14 Knife.

15 Short palette knife.

16 Long palette knife, useful for loosening cakes from baking sheets and spreading icings.

17 Dipping fork, handy for dipping fruit into chocolate.

1
2
3
4
5
6
7
8
9
10
11
12
13
14
15
16
17

13

Equipment

Although you may need to visit a specialized gourmet shop to buy some of the more unusual items of equipment shown on these pages, others are generally stocked by kitchenware stores and even supermarkets. You do not have to rush out and buy everything at once—in fact sometimes it pays to shop around in second-hand and charity shops, especially for such items as pastry cutters and icing nozzles. In this way, you can accumulate a collection of tools over a period of time, adding to your supply when you need something.

Once you have bought your equipment, it is important to store it carefully in order to prolong its life. Knives should be kept safely in a knife block, or somewhere out of children's reach where sharp blades will not be damaged by other tools, or

1 American-style cup measures.

2 Spoon measures.

3 Large ladle.

4 Mini-whisk, useful for mixing small amounts of dressing or sauces.

5 Balloon whisk, for whipping egg whites or cream.

6 Large sieve.

7 Small sieve, for sifting icing sugar and cocoa over desserts.

actually cause damage to other tools. A magnetic tool bar is a good option, although personally, I prefer to store all my sharp knives out of view in baize-lined drawers, each blade wrapped in a knife sleeve made of heavy-duty calico or canvas to protect it.

Sieves, measures, whisks, and general kitchen equipment can be easily and attractively accommodated within a couple of large containers, such as earthenware pots, placed adjacent to the stove, or suspended from a narrow tool bar screwed to the wall in a convenient place near the cooker.

Cutters, icing bags, piping nozzles and smaller pieces of equipment that can often get lost in a kitchen drawer are best kept together in small plastic boxes with sealable lids, (or even old margarine tubs) so that they can be found easily when needed.

❶ Spring-loaded butter mold.

❷ Greaseproof paper piping bag.

❸ Assorted piping nozzles.

❹ Pastry cutter.

❺ Pastry cutters.

❻ Cloth piping bag.

❼ Melon baller.

❽ Scoop for ice cream.

❾ Heart-shaped mold.

❿ Small fluted tin.

⓫ Christmas tree cookie cutter.

⓬ Assorted petits fours cutters.

⓭ Paper petits fours cups.

Raw vegetables

Decorations made from raw vegetables are easy to make and can usually be prepared well in advance and stored in the refrigerator until needed. Using everyday produce such as carrots and spring onions, and little in the way of specialized equipment, you can add a few well-chosen flourishes to just about any meal, snack, or appetizer.

Clockwise from top: *Chaud-froid* of chicken breast with red and yellow pepper flowers; sushi with a spring onion tassel; salmon quenelles with a cucumber "tulip" and chives; and a club sandwich with "rose" radishes.

Pepper flowers

Cut flowers from thin "cheeks" of raw pepper with a cookie cutter. Spring onion tips form the stalks.

Spring onion tassel

Make fine, thin cuts from the bulb upward and put the bulbs in water in the fridge until the ends curl up.

Rose radishes

Make several cuts downward to the root. Place the radish in water in the fridge until the "petals" open.

Cucumber tulip

Make cuts into cucumber halves two-thirds of the way through and bend back alternate strips.

Cooked vegetables

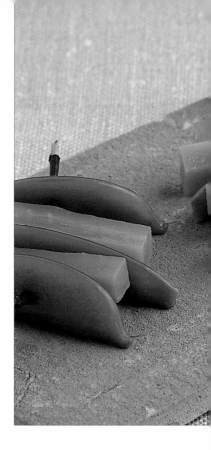

THE WONDERFUL colors and textures of vegetables provide us with endless scope for coming up with imaginative and original finishing touches to meals. And now that supermarkets offer so many ready-prepared, peeled vegetables, transforming dull, boiled carrots or beans into a visual feast takes next to no time. Not only do vegetable garnishes look good, they also contain plenty of essential nutrients—so presenting them in tempting, new ways is a good way to encourage healthy eating habits! And you can always vary the theme by using more exotic vegetables, too.

Potato balls

1 *Cut a raw potato in half and use a melon baller to extract perfect spheres of flesh.*

2 *Boil the potato balls in salted water until just cooked and serve them immediately, tossed in melted butter, sea salt, and chopped fresh mint.*

Bean bundles tied with leek ribbons

1 *Cut the outer leaves of a leek lengthwise into narrow strips, then blanch them in boiling water.*

2 *Tie the strips around 10 or so blanched, trimmed French beans and steam them until tender.*

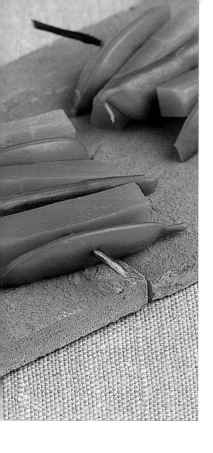

Snow peas and carrot baton "kebabs"

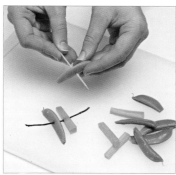 

1 *Using a cocktail stick, make guide holes through precooked carrot batons and trimmed, blanched snow peas.*

2 *Carefully thread the vegetables onto a washed, fine twig or a bamboo skewers. Steam the vegetables until tender.*

Above: Snow pea and carrot batons are easy to pass around.

Below left: Leek-tied beans.

Right: Julienned vegetables, in olive oil and chopped fresh herbs.

Below right: Diced vegetables in a bowl, with fresh chive fans.

Dicing/julienning

Root vegetables and larger vegetables such as zucchini lend themselves to this method of preparation. Cut them into fine sticks or neat cubes with a sharp vegetable knife.

Fruit

THERE ARE many ways in which fruit may be used to enhance a meal. Even very simple ideas, such as inserting a few pieces of papaya in a sliced mango, or buying and serving two different colored melons as balls alongside a platter of parma ham, give an extra element to the dish. Dramatic and attractive fruit like berries, passion fruit, and kiwis can also be used to transform a simple dish into one that is more enticing and memorable. Spicy meals in particular will benefit from the inclusion of a few carefully selected fruits, providing quite unexpected yet successful flavors.

Creating an apple garnish

1 *Using a sharp vegetable knife, cut out up to six V-shaped wedges from the side of an apple, making each wedge as uniform as possible.*

2 *Before serving, push out the wedges to form a staggered design and spritz with lemon juice.*

Above Lemon in muslin looks decorative and also makes the squeezing of juice less messy.

Below A carved apple makes a statement and gives an extra textural dimension on a tray of delicate canapés.

Top right A mango and papaya fan, with cream and cape gooseberries, makes a delicious dessert.

Below right Smoked salmon is assembled on half a lemon to form a mound, and finished off with a knotted lemon curl.

Making a mango and papaya fan

1 *Cut a series of slices from a cheek of fresh mango, then from a cheek of papaya. Try to make the slices neat and uniform.*

2 *Reassemble a cheek of the fruit, alternating the slices of mango and papaya to create a two-tone fan effect.*

Wrapping lemon in muslin

Place half a lemon, flesh down on a clean piece of muslin. Gather up the fabric and secure with string.

Making lemon curls

Use a canelli knife to pare off strips of peel, then tie a knot in each and place on a lemon or lime wedge.

Herbs

FRESH HERBS are invaluable for adding a quick and easy flourish to meals. With their attractive greenery and distinctive scents, they can enliven even the most bland of foods. From a single sprig of parsley placed on an individual canapé, to a small bunch of freshly picked herbs, gathered into a simple posy, and laid upon on a tray of delicious party snacks, herbs work their own magic. And once they are finished with as decorations, they can be chopped up and added as ingredients to a vast range of dishes, dried and sprinkled into soups, stews and casseroles, or even hung up as decorations within the home.

Useful herbs to have on hand in the garden, are variegated-leafed geraniums, colored sages, mint, and rosemary. Many everyday and more unusual herbs are now sold fresh practically all-year-round in supermarkets. Particularly handy are the pot-grown varieties, which will last for some time if kept on a windowsill and watered regularly.

Clockwise from top A herb posy adds a fragrant flourish to canapés; satay dipping sauce is served in a bay-leafed tumbler; tiny aluminium bowls of chillies, herbs, and dressing; and chives, fennel, and dill in timbale molds.

Making a herb posy

Take a few fresh herbs and arrange them into a neat posy. Tie with twine and place in water until needed.

Decorating a glass

Press several large bay leaves around a glass, so that they overlap slightly, and secure with string.

Savory sauces

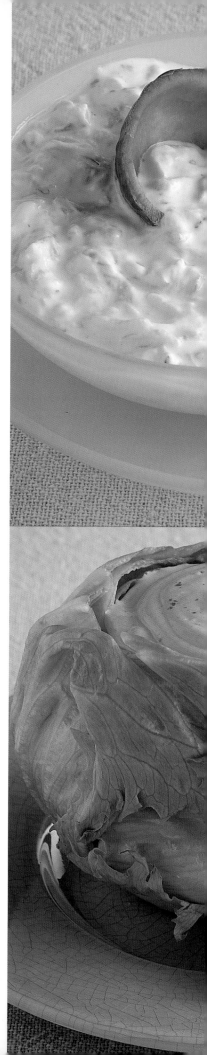

THERE ARE many ways in which store-bought sauces can be given that home-cooked touch, be it for an everyday supper or a formal occasion. Brighten up jugs and bowls by adding a few stems of herbs, or take inspiration from the sauce's ingredients to create unusual stirrers or spoons. Remember that individual portions of sauce look smarter than one huge bowl on the table.

Clockwise from top: A fresh herb stirrer adds flavor to dressing; a cucumber ladle is used to served raita; *marie-rose* sauce presented in a lettuce container; individual bowls of pesto served "on the side."

Making cucumber spoon and raita

1 *Secure a stick of celery to the hollowed-out end of a cucumber using toothpicks.*

2 *Grate a peeled cucumber and blend with garlic, sour cream or yogurt, and a little fresh mint.*

Making rosemary stirrer

Making pesto sauce

Strip lower leaves of rosemary stem, pierce garlic and chilli with a tooth-pick and thread them onto stem.

Grind fresh basil, garlic, pine nuts, and olive oil together to form a smooth paste.

Sweet sauces

Hot or cold, fruity or creamy, sweet sauces are simple to prepare and can look especially enticing when presented with care. Even canned custard takes on an extra dimension when it is served steaming hot in a traditional jug and wrapped in an attractive cloth to keep it warm. All sorts of hot sauces can be served up in this appealing manner.

If you want to make your own sweet sauce, fresh fruit coulis takes next to no time and tastes wonderful. In fact, its sharpness is ideal if you want to pep up a rather ordinary store-bought mousse or cake! Try serving Chantilly cream, or even plain whipped cream, in an attractive glass bowl draped with berries, to accompany fruit, tarts, crumbles, or similar desserts.

Above: Ready-made custard is poured into a warmed jug and wrapped in a warm napkin or clean tea cloth to keep it hot.

Left: Chocolate sauce is presented in a hollowed-out baby pineapple to accompany skewers of fresh fruit.

Top right: Raspberry coulis is served in a pretty glass jug on a saucer edged with sugar-dusted raspberries and a sprig of mint.

Opposite: Strands of fresh red currants decorate a shallow bowl of cream, placed so that they hang over its rim. The jewel-like berries look very effective against the paleness of the cream.

Making coulis

1 *Press fresh raspberries (or strawberries) through a nylon sieve into a bowl underneath, using a wooden spoon.*

2 *Add powdered sugar to the coulis mixture to sweeten it, according to your taste. Pour into a jug and chill until required.*

Making chocolate sauce

1 *Melt chocolate over a pan of boiling water and add heavy cream, stirring well. Serve immediately, or the sauce will set.*

Chocolate

ALTHOUGH THE cocoa bean was cultivated by the Incas and Aztecs of South America in the 7th century, it was not until the early 17th century that chocolate became a widespread European luxury. Courtiers and the aristocracy would consume the cocoa bean, ground to form a paste and dissolved in water, as an expensive drink. Thanks to the refinement of cocoa bean processing techniques, cakes and bars of eating chocolate began to be produced toward the end of the 19th century. Initially made of plain chocolate and sugar, milk was soon added to produce bars akin to those we know and adore to this day.

Nowadays we can buy chocolate in many forms, from the finest plain, or dark chocolate, which usually has the most intense flavor and color, to white chocolate, which is hardly chocolate at all, but instead a blend of cocoa butter, sugar, and milk that does not contain cocoa liquor, the dark and viscous paste obtained during the processing of the cocoa bean.

Plain chocolate is most commonly used for cooking because of its strong flavor and color. For the best possible taste, look for chocolate that contains a high percentage of cocoa solids—at least 34 percent. It may be more expensive but it's worth it! Chocolate-flavored cake coverings are made with a minimum of cocoa solids and although they are relatively inexpensive, they are best avoided. Their main advantage for busy cooks, however, is that they melt and set remarkably easily.

Below Milk chocolate (left) has a milder flavor, as it has full cream milk added. It can be used for icing cakes and piped onto dark chocolate as a decoration for sweets and confectionery. White chocolate (center) is ideal for making caraque curls and is often used for mousses, while dark chocolate has a depth and richness of flavor that lends itself to all manner of sauces, icings, and fillings.

Making caraque scrolls

Pour melted chocolate over a marble slab, smooth it with a knife to form a thin layer and allow to set. Push a palette knife across the chocolate to create elegant scrolls.

Above Chocolate mousses are decorated with white and dark chocolate caraques.

Left A cake is topped with dainty caraque twists.

Making caraque twists

Push a sharp knife across the layer of chocolate to create longer, but less scroll-like "tubes." This method is easier to master.

Piped chocolate

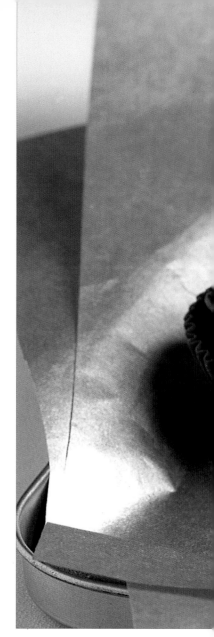

Aᴺ ᴇᴀsʏ and delicious chocolate filling can be quickly whipped up simply by melting some chocolate over a pan of hot water, and then stirring in a cube of butter, one egg yolk, and a little heavy cream. Beat the mixture well and then leave it to cool before using to fill meringues, to decorate petits fours, to pipe onto cakes or gâteaux, or to make the chocolate cups shown here. To give the chocolate filling a dash of extra flavor, you can also add a splash of brandy, or a little of your favorite liqueur.

Making chocolate cups

1 *To make the filling, melt chocolate over a pan of boiling water and then add butter, cream, and egg yolk and beat well.*

2 *Melt more chocolate and, using a spoon, coat the insides of small cupcake wrappers. Allow to set, then apply a second coat.*

3 *Place the cups in a cool place to allow the second coat of chocolate to set, then peel away the paper to reveal the chocolate cups.*

4 *Fill a piping bag, fitted with a fluted nozzle, with chocolate filling, and pipe it into the cups. Decorate as desired.*

Above Pretty chocolate cases, filled with dark and white chocolate ganache, are decorated with chocolate-dipped nuts and caraque scrolls to create delicious after-dinner treats. You could also decorate these chocolate sweets with dipped fruits, or even chocolate shapes, such as leaves (see pages 32–33).

Making a piping bag

1 *Make a rectangle (10 x 4 in.) from greaseproof paper. Fold the paper diagonally in half to form two triangular shapes.*

2 *Fold the blunt end of the triangle to create a pointed cone. Bring over the other end, making the tip as pointed as possible.*

3 *Turn in the corners at the open end of the cone and crease to secure. A paper clip or tape will keep them in place.*

31

Chocolate effects

AN EASY AND effective way to cheer up store-bought cakes or desserts is create original chocolate shapes with cookie cutters, or melt chocolate over a pan of water and then dip fruit, leaves or nuts into it. Alternatively, you can use a piping bag to create all sorts of different effects and designs.

Left and below Dipped fruit and nuts can be used to decorate desserts or they can be served with coffee as an after-dinner treat.

Chopping flakes

Break off pieces of chocolate, place them in a heat-proof bowl and melt slowly over a pan of hot water.

Creating shapes

Pour a thin layer of chocolate onto waxed paper, smooth and allow to set. Cut out your shapes.

Dipping fruit and leaves

1 *Dip individual fruits into melted chocolate that has been allowed to cool slightly. Leave to set.*

2 *Paint melted chocolate onto the undersides of clean leaves with a brush. Once set, the leaf may be carefully peeled away.*

Drizzling

Using a piping bag, drizzle cooled melted chocolate across the surface of individual cakes to create a zig-zag effect.

Writing

Fill a fine-nozzled piping bag with melted chocolate and write on baking parchment. Peel the letters carefully away from the paper.

Marbling

Drizzle melted white chocolate on dark chocolate mousse before it sets, then use a skewer to create a marbled effect.

Marzipan

A SMOOTH, MOLDABLE paste made from ground almonds, marzipan dates back to 1494, when it was known as marchpane and eaten as dainty cakes. It is easy to make your own marzipan at home, or you can buy it ready made in either white or yellow. The white variety is best if you are using a pale-colored icing.

Marzipan may also be colored to make decorative fruits and ornaments, petit-fours, and sweets.

Covering a cake

1 *Measure the depth of the cake and total length of its sides with string. Roll out the marzipan to about ¹/₄ in. thick and cut it to fit.*

2 *Brush the sides and top of the cake with warm, sieved apricot jam. Attach marzipan to the sides, aligning any edges.*

3 *Cut a piece of rolled marzipan to fit the top of the cake, transfer it on the pin and smooth any edges. Leave to dry 24 hours.*

Making shapes

Knead a little food coloring into the marzipan to achieve a uniform color. Roll out and use cookie or decorative cutters to create shapes.

"Fruits" and "veggies"

1 *Knead a few drops of food coloring, in shades such as yellow, orange, and green, into small amounts of marzipan.*

2 *Roll pieces of orange-colored marzipan into small balls, then gently roll them on a fine grater to give an "orange peel" effect. Add a clove to represent the stalk and calyx of the fruit.*

3 *Let the marzipan dry overnight, then using a fine brush and food coloring, give apples, pears, and bananas their distinct markings.*

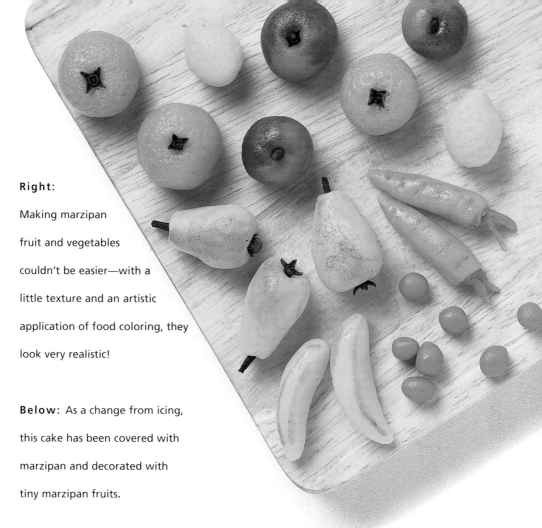

Right:

Making marzipan fruit and vegetables couldn't be easier—with a little texture and an artistic application of food coloring, they look very realistic!

Below: As a change from icing, this cake has been covered with marzipan and decorated with tiny marzipan fruits.

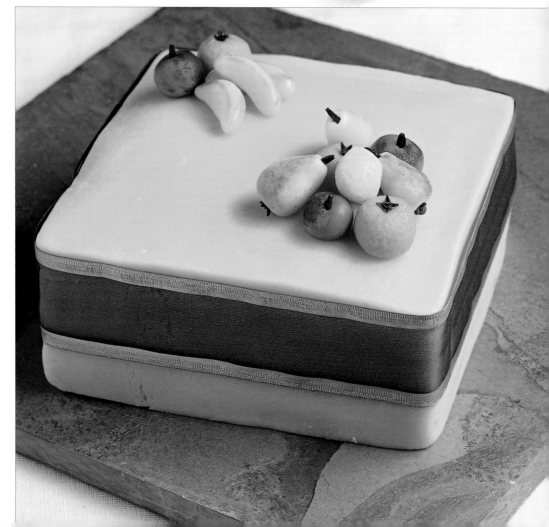

Fondant

ALTHOUGH ROYAL icing has traditionally been used to cover celebratory cakes, especially those that demand crisp sharp edges or tiers, such as wedding cakes, fondant or sugar paste is growing increasingly popular. Perhaps this is because it is much softer and simpler and so has a more contemporary look.

Fondant is easier to make than its royal counterpart, the powdered sugar being mixed in a bowl with egg whites, liquid glucose, and water or rose water. Once the mixture forms a ball, it is gently kneaded on a powdered sugar–dusted surface until it is very smooth and supple. At this stage, it may be wrapped in plastic wrap and stored for a few days until needed.

Fondant is also available in a variety of colors from specialty gourmet markets. Buying it ready-made is probably the best option if you plan to cover a large cake or several smaller ones that should all be exactly the same color.

Right: Smooth fondant covers a fruit cake, decorated with roses and leaves also made from colored fondant.

Covering the cake

1 *Roll out the fondant on a large sheet of parchment paper. Transfer fondant from work surface to cake using a rolling pin.*

2 *Dust your finger tips with cornstarch and smooth the fondant over the top and sides of the cake, removing any air bubbles.*

3 *Carefully trim around the base using a sharp knife. Dip your fingers in cornstarch, gently buff the fondant to give it gloss.*

Making a rose decoration

1 Color some fondant green, roll out a small ball and form the shape of a little sombrero. Use a cutter to create the stalk and leaf.

2 Roll out three small pieces of yellow-colored fondant to form rose-bud and attach the stalk with a little egg white.

3 Roll out small pieces of yellow fondant until paper thin, then layer them on top of one another to form a blooming rose.

Sugar dusting

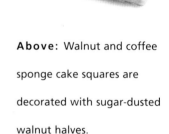

THIS IS an extremely simple way of decorating cakes and desserts, and all that's required is a little sifted powdered sugar or cocoa powder. Dramatic effects can be achieved by dredging dark cocoa powder over a large white plate, or powdered sugar on top of a rich berry sauce.

The easiest way to decorate individual desserts, such as meringues, fruit tarts, and cookies, is to use a small tea strainer, while for a larger cake, a sieve will do the trick with a couple of gentle taps. Another quick, decorative technique using sugar frosting is to place a paper doily upon the iced surface of a sponge cake, then sift powdered sugar or cocoa over the top to create a pretty stenciled effect. Carefully remove the doily, so as not to spoil the decoration and your store-bought cake will look like a million dollars.

Above: Walnut and coffee sponge cake squares are decorated with sugar-dusted walnut halves.

Left: A sifting of powdered sugar provides the finishing touch for plain and hazelnut meringues.

Top right: A cream-filled meringue is topped with a frosted cape gooseberry and served with fruit coulis on a plate dusted with powdered sugar.

Opposite: Hazelnut meringue in red-currant sauce is dredged in cocoa powder, which looks especially effective on a plain white plate.

Frosting techniques

1 *Pull back the papery cases of the cape gooseberries (also called physalis) to reveal the shiny fruits. Cover them with powdered sugar sifted through a tea strainer.*

2 *Hold the physalis carefully, so as not to spoil the powdered sugar frosting, and use a small blob of whipped cream to secure it to the meringue.*

3 *Once the dessert has been assembled, lightly frost the meringue and coulis with powdered sugar, then dust the rim of the plate.*

Crystallizing fruit & flowers

CRYSTALLIZED FRUIT looks wonderfully decorative, a coating of sugar turning the fruit into delicate pastel shades of their usual bright hues. As a finishing touch to a dessert, or an edible decoration in its own right, you can "crystallize" your own fruit and flowers by dipping them in egg white and then sprinkling sugar over them. Brightly colored and naturally attractive edible flowers and fruit lend themselves best to this elegant technique.

For fruit, use cherries, strawberries, raspberries, pretty cape gooseberries with their papery bracts still attached, or even tiny sprays of red currants. For flowers, try violets, pansies, and rose petals, as they look particularly effective when crystallized.

The fruits and flowers are lightly painted with beaten egg white and then carefully dusted with sifted sugar. Left to dry on a wire rack or sheet of waxed paper, they become crisp and will last for a day or two if stored between sheets of tissue paper in an airtight container.

Adding the frosting

1 *Ensure that the flowers (or fruit) are clean and dry. Using a fine paintbrush, lightly cover them with beaten egg white.*

2 *Spread the painted flowers (or fruit) on greaseproof paper and sprinkle sifted superfine sugar over them.*

Above: Frosted fruit and flowers in a raised opaque glass bowl makes a beautiful centerpiece that guests can help themselves to at the end of the meal.

Right: Little frosted fruits and edible flowers make the ideal garnish for summer sorbets. A few additional pieces decorate the plate.

Left: A selection of frosted fruit: strawberries, blueberries, cherries, and cape gooseberries (*physalis*).

Caramel

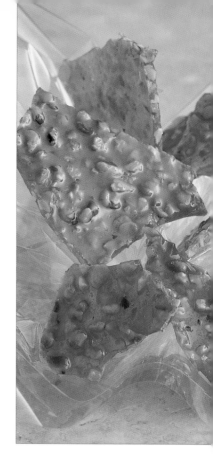

CARAMEL IS simply sugar and water which, when heated, first forms a sugary syrup, then a malleable toffee-like coating, and finally hardens into a glass-like substance. It has a mass of different uses and its warm amber coloring makes it a wonderful decoration for many desserts and cakes. To make caramel, sugar and water are stirred in a saucepan over a high heat until all the sugar is all dissolved. The syrup is allowed to boil rapidly for a few minutes and then removed from the heat, where it continues to turn amber-brown and form a caramel which may be used as soon as the bubbles have subsided.

Making caramel spikes

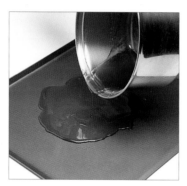

1 *Pour caramel onto an greased cookie sheet and allow it to spread into a thin, glass-like layer.*

2 *Leave the caramel to set and once hard, use a rolling pin handle to shatter it into glass-like shards. The larger shards can be used to decorate cakes or desserts.*

Making pralines

1 Mix roasted chopped nuts with the caramel. Pour the mixture onto an oiled baking sheet and use the flesh of half a lemon to smooth out the praline and add flavour.

2 The mixture will set very quickly, so while it is still malleable, use a sharp knife to divide the praline into pieces. Allow it to set before serving.

Above: Pieces of nut praline look great on clear cellophane. Wrapped, they make ideal gifts.

Left: Jagged caramel spikes make a statement atop a mousse.

Right: Caramel squiggles make a fun decoration for any dessert.

Making squiggles

Dribble caramel onto a greased cookie sheet in a haphazard fashion, to create a series of squiggly shapes. Once set, carefully life the squiggles from the tray using a palette knife.

Setting the table

THE WAY in which you lay the table sets the scene for the meal ahead, be it a simple family supper or a romantic feast. Create the atmosphere and add your own original touches by experimenting with different ways of presenting everyday items, such as napkins, cutlery, bread, butter, and condiments. With a little innovation and imagination you can transform that functional lunch, supper, or dinner party table into something really special.

Napkins

I HAVE A REAL passion for napkins, and in my own home I use one every day, with every meal I eat. Linen and damask napkins are both classic and traditional, and you can often find beautiful old linen in antique shops, markets, and second-hand shops. For modern tables, napkins and tablecloths are available in every possible color and fabric, allowing you to match and coordinate your table linen. The quality and variety of paper napkins has also greatly improved, giving you a good choice of designs at very reasonable prices. Although I prefer fabric napkins, if you are feeding a large number of people, or serving finger food, then disposable serviettes are an ideal option.

Right: The perfect way to present cutlery at a buffet dinner, this attractive bundle allows guests to pick up their cutlery and napkin in one hand.

Below: With a simple votive placed in the center, a "water lily" napkin would look charming at each place setting.

Making a water lily

1 *Fold the four corners of a starched, ironed, square napkin into the center.*

2 *Neatly fold the corners into the center again, ensuring the edges are crisp.*

3 *Turn the napkin over and fold the corners into the center again.*

4 *Pull out the corners from the bottom and open out to form "petals."*

Festive napkins

FOR THANKSGIVING and Christmas, you can decorate napkins, simply folded or rolled, with foliage, berries, and winter flowers. For buffet parties, you can pile up the napkins on plates at one end of the table, while for individual place settings you can make a separate decoration for each one.

Linen napkins in white, cream, or écru give you the most scope for decoration, since a plain background leaves you free to choose the colors to match your china. Gold and silver themes work well with most Christmas decorations, and deeper russet colors look particularly good for Thanksgiving, using whatever berries and autumn leaves you can find in your yard. A sprig or two is all that is needed, coupled with some attractive ribbons.

Wired ribbons tie and drape particularly well and avoid the need for complicated bows. The simpler the decoration, the more effective it looks, so keep the ribbons and trimmings to a minimum. Candlelight will help to add atmosphere, so do bear this in mind when planning the table decorations (see Setting the Style, pages 60–75).

Right: Christmas napkins tied with gold wire ribbon, and decorated with sprigs of holly leaves and berries.

Below: Napkins tied with dark red ribbon, houttynia leaves, and rose hips.

Left: Napkins for an autumn celebration dinner, piled up together with the top one decorated with brown silk ribbon, clematis seed heads, rose hips, and honeysuckle berries.

Napkins as containers

Napkins make wonderful containers for serving food such as bread, dry fruit, vegetables, salads, crackers, and cheeses. I find them especially useful when entertaining large numbers of people since they are quickly transformed into attractive bowls and baskets when you have run out of crockery and chinaware!

Right: Jewel-like cherry tomatoes on the vine, nestle inside a simply knotted leaf-green napkin. Placed on a board, they may be offered to guests at a picnic or *al fresco* luncheon.

Left: A whole stilton cheese, with top crust removed, wrapped within a large natural linen napkin, brings a traditional serving idea up-to-date.

Right: French bread can look rather dull if it is simply sliced and piled into a basket or bowl. To make the most of its crusty charm, why not slice it and reassemble the loaf in a rolled napkin, folded lengthwise and secured at each end with handmade "clothespins."

Novel containers

GIVE MEALS a novel twist by doing away with everyday dishes. Many vegetables and other organic materials are easily transformed into bowls or containers, in which you may serve salads, sauces, dips, and desserts in a dramatic way. Surprise your guests with imaginative presentation and the meal will be successful, even if you bought the food ready-made!

Clockwise from top right: Guacamole in deseeded peppers; asian dipping sauces served in hollow stems of fresh green bamboo; sorbets in a fresh pineapple; and stir-fried noodles and shrimp in banana-leaf bowls.

Making the banana-leaf bowl

1 *Cut a circle from a fresh banana leaf. Pinch two sides together, skewer and tie with raffia thread.*

2 *Turn the leaf by a quarter, pinch, and secure with raffia again. Repeat for two more corners.*

Making the pineapple bowl

1 *Take a slice from one side of the fruit so that it sits stably. Cut a third from the other side.*

2 *Cut around the inside edge of the skin to loosen the flesh, then scoop it out with a spoon.*

Bread

Whether you are serving a store-bought baguette, a homemade loaf, or run-of-the-mill sliced toast, bread may be a daily staple but it need never look ordinary. Opt for loaves with interesting seeds, herbs, or flavorings, and present it in interesting ways to make the most of its texture and color.

Right: A basket created from stems of dried wheat, bound at the corners with raffia, and lined with a torn square of calico, is an appropriate natural container for chunks of rustic bread.

Left: Biscuit cutters are used to make rings of bread which are then toasted under a grill, threaded onto a skewer and served with marmalade. These would also be an excellent accompaniment to pâtés and other canapés or snacks, arranged either on a platter or a skewer, and served with butter.

Right: Small terra-cotta pots are used as molds for baking individual loaves. The bread should be cooked well in advance so that the loaves can be removed from the molds and allowed to cool. The pots can then be reheated and the loaves reinserted to warm up just before serving.

Making the bread basket

1 Attach the ends of two bundles of dried wheat to form a right angle. Attach a third bundle at the head with raffia or twine.

2 Add another layer of wheat bundles, heads above stem ends. Tie with raffia, trim, and line the basket with calico or a napkin.

Butter

Smooth, golden, and extremely malleable, butter lends itself to a wide variety of decorative treatments—so although it may be an everyday staple, butter need never look ordinary. One simple effect is achieved by running the tines of a table fork across the surface of a slab of butter, first lengthways, then across the width, to create a rough, trammeled effect. Another treatment is simply to cut well-chilled butter into small, neat cubes, and pile them up in a shallow bowl or saucer, placing a single fresh herb stem alongside. In fact, with a little imagination, you can mold butter into just about any shape or form you like!

Below: Softened butter is placed in a ramekin, swirled with a palette knife, and topped with a fresh herb; firm butter is formed into traditional curls; soft butter is mixed with fresh herbs, rolled and sliced; and a slab of butter is shaped in an attractive French wooden mold, which may be extravagant but is visually worth every penny!

Using a butter mold

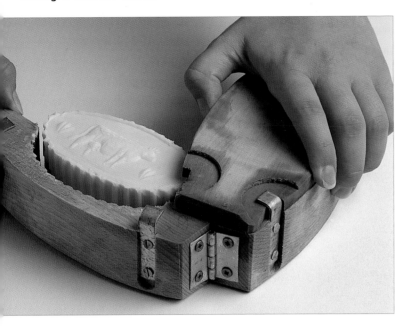

1 Wet the butter mold and fill it with softened butter, packing it into every corner and crevice. Chill.

2 Once chilled, ease the butter out of the mold so as not to spoil the pattern with your fingers.

Creating butter curls

Run a butter-curling tool down a chilled slab of butter. Store curls in iced water in the fridge until needed.

Making herb butter

Swirling butter

Use a palette knife in a spiralling, paddling action to create the swirls.

1 Beat softened butter in a bowl until smooth. Stir in fresh, finely chopped mixed herbs.

2 Place the mixture on waxed paper or foil and roll into a sausage shape. Chill the butter before cutting it into slices.

Salt and pepper

Top chefs might have us believe that it is not necessary to place condiments on the table, but I always put out salt and pepper, and if appropriate, mustard, even if it is a simple supper in the kitchen. For everyday meals, salt and pepper mills are fine, but for a special occasion or to give an extra decorative touch, you can easily and quickly create plenty of containers. Naturally hollow vegetables, such as gourds, are excellent when filled with good, strong English mustard as the colors complement one another so well. Large nonpoisonous leaves can be formed into cones secured with cocktail sticks and filled with salt and pepper. Miniature terra-cotta pots, glass votive holders and vases may all be filled with seasonings, as can shells, shallow saucers, and little trays or bowls.

Right: These miniature galvanized buckets make the perfect holders for salt, pepper, and mustard. Here, cracked pepper is used, as it slightly coarser than milled pepper and has a more intense flavor. It also lends itself to an informal outdoor meal, as do the buckets.

Middle: Scallop shells make pretty, practical salt and pepper holders. To prevent their rounded bases from wobbling about, they are placed on a folded napkin to keep them stable.

Left: Edible leaves can be formed into cones and held in place with a cocktail stick or toothpick. They make the perfect partners for a miniature pumpkin filled with mustard.

Below: Salt and pepper have been poured into a small terra-cotta saucer divided by a curved index card. When the card is then removed, it leaves the condiments attractively separated in this swirling, yin-yang shape.

Setting the style

THERE ARE TIMES when you wish to celebrate a birthday, perhaps, or commemorate an anniversary with a special meal—be it breakfast in bed, an intimate dinner for two, or a family celebration. How you present the food depends on how formal, or informal, the occasion is to be. The important element is to ensure that the food, the setting, and the accessories—table linen, cutlery, and glassware—all harmonize in some way.

Breakfast

THERE IS nothing quite like a traditional cooked breakfast, and although few of us linger over such a meal every morning, many appreciate a leisurely brunch over the weekend. For those who love the idea and aroma of a cooked breakfast but don't want to indulge in a heavy, cholesterol-laden meal, a beautifully presented mini-breakfast is the ideal alternative. When accompanied by toast and marmalade, even the heartiest of eaters should have little cause for complaint. The alternative for fish lovers is kedgeree, a light English breakfast dish of rice, fresh fish (haddock is traditional), and eggs with spices.

Right: A strip of bacon, hash brown, fried quail's egg, grilled cherry tomatoes, and toast are served with a chilled Virgin or Bloody Mary.

Below: Kedgeree was a well-loved Victorian breakfast dish. Today it is a lighter alternative to fried foods and may be made with all types of fish.

Lunch

WHETHER you are hosting an informal lunch with friends or simply sitting down with the family, making a little extra effort to decorate the table really pays dividends. Spring and summer call for fresh and fragrant decorations, such as this lemon and lime pyramid, which relies upon the textures and form of the fruit, foliage, and flowers used within it for its dramatic effect.

The base of the decoration is a store-bought cone of dried flower foam, onto which fresh green mounds of baby's tears, lemons, limes, and purple lilac are wired, using florist's stub wires. Citrus fruits are ideal for this centerpiece since they have a tough skin and are easy to wire into position. Once you have finished with the decoration, you can even use the fruit to make jam or marmalade, so that nothing goes to waste. A more permanent version could be created using the same technique but replacing the fresh fruit with pine cones, artificial or preserved fruits and vegetables, which should then be wired onto the cone and dried mosses used to fill any gaps.

Opposite This contemporary decoration is created using sprigs of baby's tears, halved lemons and limes, and stems of purple lilac, the colors of which are echoed in the table linen.

Making the cone

1 *Loosely cover a flower foam cone with sprigs of baby's tears, fixing it with "hairpins" of bent lengths of florist's wire.*

2 *Push stub wires through the whole or halved fruits and twist them onto themselves to form a support, then insert into foam.*

3 *Fix a more sprigs of baby's tears and wired purple lilac between the fruits, then spray with water to keep fresh.*

Left During colder months, make use of autumnal fruits and leaves, and arrange them around candles in imaginative ways. In this way you can create decorations that will bring warmth and color to the table in a matter of minutes.

Afternoon tea

W**HEN TIME ALLOWS**, there is nothing quite so luxurious than sitting down to a delicious, traditional afternoon tea, served with the English ceremony and style for which it is renowned. It provides the perfect excuse to dust off old tea sets, or to use odd bone china cups and saucers, which are so often embellished with pretty flowers and leaves. Such motifs may inspire a floral theme for the meal, as here, where fresh violets have been crystallized to decorate the cupcakes, and tied in a bouquet to adorn the coffee cake. Cucumber sandwiches are a mainstay of this meal, presented as temptingly dainty triangles.

Making cucumber sandwiches

1 *Thinly slice a cucumber and sprinkle with salt to draw out the moisture and prevent the sandwiches from becoming soggy.*

2 *Remove the crusty end of a whole-wheat loaf and spread softened butter thinly over the bread.*

3 *Cut a fine slice from the loaf and remove all crusts. Butter more bread and slice as necessary.*

Right: The vital ingredients of a traditional afternoon tea are presented on fine bone china and a silver and glass cake stand upon a floral embroidered cloth and served, of course, with plenty of freshly brewed tea .

Japanese theme

THERE IS SOMETHING particularly appealing about the way in which food is served in the East. Although I often advocate over-the-top decorative style, I also appreciate the minimalist, uncluttered presentation of neatly wrappped sushi or exquisite slivers of freshest sashimi, adorned with a single orchid or beautifully carved vegetable. Recreating this look could not be simpler since very few elements are needed to complement the food.

If you do not wish to serve an entire Japanese meal, look out for Asian snacks and appetizers in the ready-made section of most good supermarkets. The supermarket sushi ranges make attractive and easy cold snacks or starters, with both vegetarian and fish choices available.

You can sometimes find traditional Japanese lacquerware in second-hand shops, where one-of-a-kind platters, plates, and bowls can be had for bargain prices. If you can't find a suitable tray, you may improvise by placing a simple bamboo place mat on an everyday plate or tray and adding a few flowers alongside the food.

Left: A small mat is made from lengths of green "snake grass," which resembles fresh bamboo, and is a perfect way to present jasmine tea.

Right: Sushi is served with style on a simple tray, which sits on a banana leaf.

Caribbean

I N THIS striking setting, banana leaves and lush tropical foliage and fruits are combined with brightly colored flowers, china, glassware, and linen to recreate a colorful Caribbean theme. This would be an ideal setting for an outdoor summer party, or even a dinner party during winter to remind us of warmer, sunny days. Create some exotic fresh fruit salads and use fresh coconuts and mini-bananas as decorative elements—fortunately these are edible too.

Above and below: Strips of banana leaf formed into cones, secured with toothpicks, and stuck into half a tangerine make a cruet set, while a halved coconut contains halved kumquats around a votive candle.

Right: Banana leaves, coconut, tropical fruit evoke a Caribbean scene.

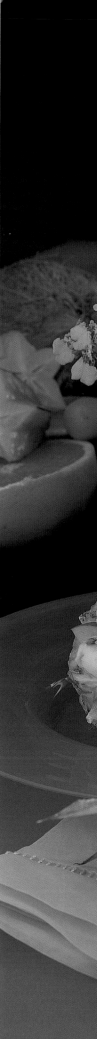

Mexican fiesta

THE HOT-COLORED chili peppers and the bold shapes of succulent plants in contemporary containers that form this themed table setting immediately bring to mind the tempestuous excitement of Latin America. Unusual succulent plants will last for years with very little attention, and for this decoration they have merely been gently removed from their existing pots and placed together within a shallow glass bowl. The lining of fresh chili peppers adds an element of color and texture and evokes a feeling of spiciness and heat. Table linen, glasses, and crockery have been carefully chosen to enhance and blend in with the whole setting, while smooth, rounded stones, each topped with a single chili are scattered around the table, evoking a sense of the desert and adding contemporary chic to the setting.

Left A large red bell pepper makes an interesting, fun container for a single succulent plant. Red chili peppers add the finishing touch.

Right Enchiladas and guacamole are served at this Mexican-style supper, where vibrant chili peppers give as much visual spice to the setting as they do to the cuisine.

Indian buffet

FOODS THAT contain rich, colorful ingredients really lend themselves to the full decorative treatment. Choose exotic containers for such dishes, and you can make them look dramatic and original, even if the food arrived at your door in telltale to-go containers! With the aid of vibrant fabrics, flowers, and spices, you can be as flamboyant as you wish in presenting an Indian meal. Brilliant colored silks are inexpensive to buy from Indian sari shops, and each sari length makes a generous tablecloth. Try combining a couple in very different shades, using one as a base cloth and the other swathed across the table. Place little brass, copper, or earthenware pots and bowls and tiny candles set in miniature terra-cotta bowls among the fabric, then complete the scene with a scattering of marigold and rose petals alongside bowls of dahl, vegetarian curry, and cool lassi drinks.

Left: Small brass finger bowls are scented with sliced fresh limes, star anise and marigold petals. Warm water will help to release the essential oils of the fruit and spices, producing a fragrant and refreshing mixture.

Right Tall glasses of lassi are placed on a colorful table, heaped with elements of Indian style. Rich swathes of bright but inexpensive sari silks are draped across the table. Among them, large brass platters and bowls are positioned, full of fragrant rice, delectable curries, and naan bread fresh from the oven. With loads of tiny candles and strewn flower petals, the Indian subcontinent seems so much nearer!

Everyday meals

P REPARING AND serving the daily meal is probably part of your routine but that does not have to encourage monotony. In fact, presenting everyday staples in new and different ways is as stimulating for the chef as it is for the diners! Even if you are serving ready-made meals, with a little imagination and know-how you can give them the added appeal of your own personal touch.

Starters

SERVING UP a three-course meal used to involve spending hours in the kitchen. Fortunately, that is no longer the case, especially since supermarkets have so many ready-made offerings that need only a little primping and preening to look and taste impressive. Save yourself time by buying prepared salads and vegetables: all you have to think about is choosing the right ingredients and putting them together with panache.

Serving a cold starter is by far the easiest option, as, on the whole, it may be prepared several hours in advance and will survive in the fridge until you are ready to eat. The other bonus is that you can relax and spend more time with your guests without having to keep disappearing into the kitchen!

I always endeavor to serve a cold starter if I am attempting to cook a rather complex main course because it leaves me free to devote all my care and time to ensuring the success of the main dish without having to keep darting between various pots and pans. If you are cooking in a small kitchen with minimal facilities, it is also important to give yourself plenty of room to prepare for the main course.

Right: Single leaves of baby lettuce are used as containers for Caesar salad, which is scattered with crisp croutons and shavings of parmesan cheese.

Below: Small spheres of avocado and mozzarella are scooped out with a melon baller and arranged in a hollowed out beefsteak tomato.

Right: A slice of smoked salmon is formed into a rose by simply rolling the slice onto itself. The tips of its "petals" are dipped into fresh, finely chopped parsley before being served on a bed of salad leaves.

Starters

MANY STORE-BOUGHT soups and delicatessen pâtés are as good as homemade versions, certainly if given a little crafty help and presented in an original fashion. Mix in a little fresh cream or a small drop of brandy or other appropriate ingredient as you warm up your can or carton of soup, and no one will guess that you have not made it yourself. Slabs of pâté from the delicatessen always tend to look rather ugly and processed, but by cutting them into smaller and more delicate portions they immediately become appetizing and acceptable.

When choosing fish as a starter, why not opt for small fillets of smoked mackerel, halibut, or herring, as these are easily presented with mouth-watering effect by adding a few salad leaves and an interesting, but easily concocted, accompaniment. When selecting the menu, bear in mind the color of the plates or bowls you will be using. Creamy chicken soup served in a shallow white or cream bowl will look bland and rather uninteresting, whereas in a deep blue or green bowl, garnished with chopped fresh herbs, it would instantly have more appeal.

Right: A quenelle of mascarpone cheese blended with creamed horseradish is the accompaniment to smoked mackerel fillets, garnished with watercress.

Below: Lobster bisque is poured into warmed soup bowls and a disk of chilled bought puff-pastry is placed on top before being cooked in the oven until well risen. The pastry crust makes a nice change from the usual bread roll .

Right: A pastry cutter is used to extract this "drum" shape from a thick slice of store-bought smooth pâté. Each drum is spread with prepared Chinese plum sauce and finished with a flourish of orange rind.

Meat

EAT IS one of the most difficult foods to present well at the table. All too often it can look rather brown and unappetizing, particularly if it is a large joint or has been stewed in a casserole. Yet when presented in the right way, meat can look wonderfully appealing: who—other than a vegetarian, of course—could resist a perfectly cooked and presented steak? I think that the trick is to present slightly smaller portions to your guests, while giving them the option of having seconds. Rather than giving my guests too large a helping, I would rather allow people to choose to how much or little they wish to eat.

Remember, too, that a few stems of a fresh green herb or a bright tomato or vegetable will always add an element of decoration to a rather brown or beige palette.

Right: A mini version of chicken-in-the-basket, succulent fried catfish on a pile of steak-fries, served in a tiny basket.

Above: A juicy grilled steak is presented on a crunchy crust of bread, the whole moistened with a pat of fresh herb butter

Opposite: Spring lamb cutlets carved from a well-cooked crown or rack of lamb are positioned so that they support each other as a tripod, upon a bed of tasty flageolet beans.

Fish

Easy to prepare, quick to cook, low in fat and high in protein, fish is more than simply delicious. Large and well-stocked fish counters and markets provide a huge and colorful choice of fish and shellfish from all around the world, so it makes perfect sense to serve fish at least once or twice a week.

For good value and flavor, cod fillets are difficult to beat. Given a light seasoning, seared on the skin side in a hot pan for 20 seconds, then roasted in a hot oven for 10 minutes and served on a mound of pesto mashed potatoes accompanied by a salad, they make a wonderful meal.

Fresh shellfish may also be incorporated into delicious meals. Large bowls of *moules marinières* or platters of freshly shucked oysters served on a bed of ice, and with fresh bread and salad are two particular favorites. Do remember however, that it is imperative that shellfish are as fresh as possible. If you are in any doubt, it is best to avoid them.

Braiding fish

1 *Take one skinless fillet of salmon and one of flounder and, using a sharp knife, slice them lengthwise into four strips.*

2 *Twist the strips of fish around one another to form a neat twist and secure with a skewer or toothpick during cooking.*

Right Fresh oysters are presented on a platter of crushed ice, garnished with samphire—an edible salt water marsh grass—and lemon wedges.

Left Steamed twists of salmon and flounder are served with a traditional parsley sauce and steamed cucumber.

Vegetables

VEGETABLES ARE extremely important in our daily diet—we eat so many of them, yet we rarely present them with the style and panache that they deserve. Those pale, dull-looking florets of boiled cauliflower and uninspiring chopped carrots, straight from the saucepan, can look temptingly presentable with a little forethought and inspiration.

Making the most of vegetables is as much about coming up with interesting combinations of color, shape, and texture as it is with preparing, chopping, slicing, or dicing vegetables in more unusual ways. Next time you happen to visit the produce or farmers' market, or even the vegetable department of the supermarket, ascertain what is in season or what appears to be particularly fresh and colorful. By choosing the freshest or the most appealing vegetables, you are already half-way to producing a visual feast.

Miniature vegetables always look wonderful, and although they may be rather more expensive than their larger counterparts, they do make a change from the norm. Colorful vegetable purées also take little time to prepare and can be presented in dramatic patterns. Adding a few fresh chopped herbs provides a much-needed color contrast when serving some of the blander vegetables. Potatoes, in particular, will always benefit from a different treatment since they often look predictable and unexciting.

Clockwise from top Spinach molds, topped with toasted breadcrumbs and pine nuts; tender green asparagus spears, scattered with parmesan shavings and drizzled with olive oil; and a platter of miniature steamed vegetables, chosen for their different shapes and colors and sprinkled with fresh, chopped herbs.

Salads

WITH so many exotic and colorful leaves, all shapes and sizes of tomatoes, and myriad other ingredients now being tossed into inventive salads, long gone are the days when a few limp lettuce leaves and slices of cucumber could thus be described. Salads are no longer the "boring" or healthy option, but are delicious meals in their own right. There are now wonderful ingredients available all year round, and although the unusual leaves are more expensive, just a few of them can put real life and soul into a large bowl of inexpensive greenery. If you are lucky enough to have a garden, or even a windowbox, try growing your own leaves or edible flowers, so that your salad ingredients are close at hand. Rice and pasta salads are inexpensive and filling, but often look dull. By adding a few handfuls of wild rice to the pan, or cooking different shaped or colored pastas together, these take on a new look. Think about the colors of your salad ingredients, and remember that less is often more. A rice salad with a couple of well-chosen added ingredients for example, looks far more appetizing than one which contains so many extras that both the eye and the palate are confused!

Right A wine glass has been used as the mould for a dramatic rice salad made from a blend of wild and long grain rice, disks of green pepper, peeled fava beans, a little flavored oil, and fresh chives.

Below Classic tomato, basil, and mozzarella salad is presented in a regimented and minimalist fashion on a dramatically colored plate.

Left Baby salad leaves are combined with some more ordinary lettuce leaves. Dressed in the traditional style, the whole dish is garnished with a flourish of edible flower heads.

Potatoes

XCEEDINGLY VERSATILE, inexpensive, and immensely satisfying, it is little wonder that potatoes are such popular fare. Across the world, they are prepared in myriad different styles and used in countless recipes, yet they taste just as good on their own, baked in the oven and served in their "skins." Nowadays, potatoes are available in all shapes and forms from the freezer section of most supermarkets: whether you want fries or fritters, you no longer have to slave over the sink with a potato peeler! Potatoes may be an everyday staple, but they can also provide an element as part of any meal, be it a weekday supper or an elaborate formal dinner. They also vary according to the season, from the large, floury baking potatoes of autumn to waxy winter potatoes that are excellent for french fries and roasting, to tiny marble-sized new potatoes in late spring and summer that are so delicious when cooked with fresh mint and served with melted butter and freshly chopped herbs.

Clockwise from top New potatoes are cooked in the oven in buttered waxed paper; fries are tossed in salt and presented in a newspaper cone; rutabaga and herbed mashed potatoes are served in a layered stack.

Making a rutabaga and potato stack

1 *Spoon mashed potato and chives into the base of a tube cut from a plastic drink bottle.*

2 *Spoon well-drained mashed rutabaga on top, and layer potato and rutabaga alternately.*

Fruit and cheese

THERE IS NO BETTER way to finish a meal than with cheese and fruit. It makes the perfect final touch, particularly when presented with style. You do not need to make the presentation elaborate, but it is important to choose platters that marry well with the ingredients.

How you present fruit depends on the type and the season. Summer fruits are more brightly colored and tend to look good in glass bowls. Autumn fruits, in rich russets, deep plums, and guinea golds, require a warmer treatment. Using foliage and flowers as a decoration works well. Foliage is particularly appropriate for cheeses, which are traditionally served on a bed of vine leaves. Purple and green sage leaves, with their soft bloom, also look good with the pale creams of most cheeses. If using flowers as decorations for fruit, pick colors that harmonize well—deep blues with purple and red fruit, bright oranges with yellow and reds, for example.

Right: A cheese platter, served on cool marble, covered in vine leaves, with grapes and pomegranates. The simple cheese boxes and waxed papers add a natural touch.

Left: Deep purple and red late summer and autumn fruits are served with foliage as decoration.

Desserts

WHEN TIME is short, you can quickly enhance bought mousse and cheesecake mixes by adding a drop or two of flavoring or liqueur; make a bought cake look extra special by slicing it into smaller, elegant wedges, or give a gâteau a homemade feel by cutting it into squares. Frozen desserts are ideal for this treatment as they can be sliced while semi-frozen.

Clockwise from top A lemon mousse is drizzled with melted chocolate; cheesecake is served on feathered sauce; mousse made from a packet mix is served in an espresso cup, and chocolate cake is given a stencil effect.

Creating a feathered effect

1 *Pour chocolate sauce into a shallow dish and use a teaspoon to drop cream around the edge.*

2 *Draw a skewer or toothpick out from the center of each blob of cream to "feather" it.*

Using a stencil decoration

1 *Draw a pattern onto a piece of stiff card, then cut out your design with scissors or a craft knife.*

2 *Place the stencil on a piece of gâteau, sprinkle over sugar or cocoa, and remove stencil carefully.*

Desserts

DESSERTS MADE from fresh fruits are generally very popular and can be easily made to look wonderful, as the simple beauty and colors of fruit effectively do most of the the job for you! Look out for small cartons of out-of-season berries flown in from overseas since these always make store-bought fruit tartlets look extra special, or give a touch of color and luxury to an easily made fruit salad. Many shops now sell delicious pastry cases and even fluted tart cases, which, when filled with whipped cream, fruits, and berries, look and taste marvelous. Give your fruity desserts an extra flourish by adding a sprig of fresh mint or other edible leaf or flower and a dredging of icing sugar or cocoa. This will give the impression that hours have been spent in the kitchen.

Right Brandy snap baskets, filled with cream and fruit and served on fruit coulis.

Below right Fruit tartlets are glazed with warm red-currant jelly and decorated with strawberry leaves.

Below Pineapple and kiwi chunks, which have been marinaded in a bowl of cinnamon and star-anise-flavored sugar syrup, are served on skewers.

Petits fours

IF YOU WANT TO give the afternoon tea table a special touch, you can dress up some shop-bought cakes with ready-made fondant, a pretty ribbon or two, and some delicate edible frosted flowers (see pages 40–41)—pansies, violets, rose petals, and primroses are all ideal. A Battenberg cake, for example, can be cut into square-sized pieces and covered with the fondant. A single flower is enough to adorn the top of each cake—if you are making a batch of them they will last for several days as the sugar preserves them.

It is a good idea to color the fondant to match the colors of the flowers you are using. Be warned—a little coloring goes a very long way so add it drop by drop until you achieve the color you want.

The little cakes would also make an excellent edible gift for a family anniversary or party, especially if you put each one into a pretty, personalized box, with the initial of the recipient stenciled on the lid.

Far right: Pretty ribbons in pastel shades decorate the cakes.

Right and clockwise: A pansy, diascias, and primulas are all embellished with a delicate rock geranium leaf.

Cupcakes and pastries

HERE ARE times when we have all been offered plates of cookies and pastries that look like they have just been dumped out of a cardboard box. Yet, even if you have no intention of baking your own pastries, you need never fall into the trap of presenting unappetizing ones. With a little ingenuity and a few interesting and attractive items of glass or chinaware, such as a platter or cake stand, all sorts of pastries can be made to look pretty, elegant, and delicious. Unusual cake stands can often be found at bargain prices in second-hand shops, and they will give an instant lift, quite literally, to anything served on them. Large trays and plates are also useful for offering around individual pastries and sweetrolls. To disguise an old tray or a chipped plate, you can always cover it with a sheet of colored tracing paper or a pretty lace cloth.

Below Traditional iced cupcakes are decorated with crystallized flowers and presented on a simple glass cake stand. The stand is covered with a star-shaped doily cut from a sheet of pastel shaded tracing paper, the color of which complements the pretty icing on the cakes. A sprinkling of silver stars completes the effect.

Left Store-bought tartlets are given extra impact by being presented on the large, uncluttered surface of a tea tray. The pastries are all given space and positioned in neat rows, which allows their dramatic colors and forms to be appreciated far more than if they were all cluttered together on a small plate.

Right Two different flavored cakes are sliced into equal-sized portions and then reassembled alternately to form what looks like one cake, but with a striking duo-tone effect. This extremely simple but effective presentation idea works best when the flavors of the two cakes chosen complement one another. Here, the sharpness of lemon enhances the sweetness of chocolate.

Cookies and candies

1 *Take a square-shaped sheet of stiff card. First, fold it in half in each direction, and then fold it diagonally into triangles.*

At the conclusion of a good meal, it is always a real treat to be offered delicious chocolates and cookies along with coffee. These tiny biscuits and sweetmeats are now readily available from many shops and supermarkets, but although tasty, these often look as though they have been mass produced, which rather spoils the effect. It is, however, an easy and straight-forward process to give them added panache and present them in a far more imaginative fashion.

Small tartlets and miniature cakes look wonderful when placed on a simple glass platter or traditional cake stand, either on a simple store-bought paper doily or, for a more contemporary look, upon a couple of different colored sheets of glassine paper. To offer chocolates to your guests in a more interesting and imaginative way, why not try making a very simple container from a square of stiff paper or card, secured at the corners with cord or twine. Fill the paper bowl with petit fours and then sit it on a rush table mat that has been scattered with chocolates and cocoa powder.

2 *Using a sharpened pencil point or a skewer, carefully pierce a hole in the corner of each folded triangle.*

Above and left Miniature tartlets are stacked on glassine paper draped over a cake stand; store-bought chocolate shapes make attractive decorations.

Opposite A container is made by folding stiff paper, securing it with cord, and lining it with purple glassine paper. The bowl is offered around on a rush paper mat strewn with chocolate shapes and cocoa powder.

3 *Use cord or string to bring the four corners together, forming the sheet of paper into a small shallow box.*

Children's meals

WITH mimimum effort, children's meals can be transformed into fun and exciting experiences. You can encourage youngsters to eat more healthfully by appealing to their natural inquisitiveness. Even a "boring" sandwich filling will become irresistible if the bread has been cut into the shape of a favorite animal or character, while skewers of fruit and vegetables look fun, too. With such good habits formed, the occasional sweet or treat will do no harm at all!

Fruity juices

IN TRYING TO STEER children away from sickly sweet, sugary drinks, a little imagination can work wonders. If they look fun and colorful, even healthy fruit juices can appeal to younger tastes. Fresh watermelon, liquidized and sweetened with a little sugar syrup and puréed raspberries, makes a delicious and exotic drink for children. Served on a "tray" of sliced watermelon in glasses decorated with chunks of the fruit, it looks irresistible. Alternatively, you might use fruit on sticks to make glasses of their favorite drinks look extra special. Colored ice cubes are always a favorite, brightening up everyday orange or apple juice.

Top left: Served on a watermelon platter, this fruity drink is sure to be a hit with the youngsters.

Left: Blueberries and strawberries on a stick and a piece of lime add a splash of color to an orange drink.

Below and far right: Dyed with a touch of food coloring and stored in the freezer, these pink, yellow, and red ice cubes are ideal for brightening up children's party drinks. If made from strawberry, lemon, or other fruit drinks, such as black currant or lime, they can also be served up as mini-Popsicles.

Fun sandwiches

Y OU WILL be amazed at how popular even plain sandwich fillings become when served in appealing, fun ways. Pinwheel swirls of chocolate spread are a permissible treat when presented alongside open ham sandwiches cut into pig shapes, and flowers and stars cut from a variety of flavored open sandwiches using simple pastry and cookie cutters. If you find it hard to persuade children to eat more healthily on a daily basis, try presenting everyday staples in new shapes and sizes to make meal times more fun.

Making boats

1 *Slice off the bottom of a bridge roll, so that the "hull" of the boat is flat. Spread the cut halves with butter or margarine.*

2 *Spread on your sandwich mix so that it looks smooth. Add strips of bell pepper and tomato slices to decorate the boat.*

3 *Cut a square of American cheese in half and thread onto a cocktail stick to make a sail.*

Right: Pig-shaped ham-and-cheese sandwiches are given "eyes" of bell pepper. Bite-sized sandwiches, cut out using petits fours cutters, are speared on skewers and stuck into a halved melon. Jam sandwiches are far more appealing when shaped like flowers and stars.

Veggies

ENCOURAGING YOUNG children to eat vegetables as part of their daily diet can be inordinately difficult. With the temptations of so many sweets, fizzy drinks, and junk and fast foods designed to appeal to younger appetites, vegetables tend to come way down the list of children's favorite foods.

Yet even if you find it impossible to persuade your youngster to eat a Brussels sprout or parsnip because of its strong flavor, there are many everyday vegetables that children do enjoy, if they can be tempted to at least try them in the first place.

With very little effort, you can transform dull piles of carrot, mounds of peas, or slices of cucumber into something altogether more appetizing and interesting. Take your inspiration from kids' favorite story books or cartoon films and use your imagination to create shapes, animals, or objects that will grab their attention. Keep the more fiddly or time-consuming ideas for special occasions, while other simple vegetable shapes can be prepared in advance and then cooked along with the adult fare, so that you do not spend any longer in the kitchen than necessary.

Right Perfect for a special occasion, this train will prove a hit with children. Its carriages are filled with assorted dips, cubes of colorful red pepper, and other crudités.

Below Goldfish are cut from thick slices of raw carrot using a pastry cutter or template and then cooked. Peas add the final 'bubble' flourish.

Left Grated carrot is piled into hollowed-out cucumber, which has a cucumber sail and radish and celery oars. For a cooked version, use zucchini, peas or mashed potatoes as the filling, and green beans as oars.

Novelty Jell-O

THIS FUN idea is a real favorite with younger children and is straightforward and relatively quick to create. I have used a pair of square flower vases which, having been thoroughly cleaned, are ideal as a makeshift fish "tanks." You may, of course, use any suitable glass or even plastic container, provided it will hold a quantity of warm liquid.

Small hard candies are sprinkled in a shallow layer at the base the container to look like "gravel" at the bottom of the tank. A layer of cooled gelatin liquid is then poured over the top, and allowed to set in a cool place, or in the refrigerator.

Once set, slim sprigs of fresh rosemary are inserted into the layer of jelly, to resemble seaweed. At this stage, goldfish shapes and those of other underwater creatures can be cut out from chunks of set, firm gelatin and added to the tank. Once the shapes are in position, the container is topped up with more cooled liquid gelatin and allowed to set. Finally, a small sailing boat, also made from gelatin, is placed on the surface of the edible aquarium, looking just as though it is "floating" across the water.

Above Juicy raspberries and blueberries look wonderful set in near-transparent gelatin, cut out in fun shapes that children will love.

Right The perfect aquarium for youngsters with a sweet tooth, this Jell-O scene would go down well at a tea party.

Making the jelly fish

1 *Mix gelatin, using less water than usual, pour into a shallow tray, leave to set. Cut out jelly fish using a template made from card.*

Making the jelly boats

1 *Slice an orange in half and scoop out the fruit. Pour gelatin mixture into each half and allow to set.*

2 *Cut orange halves into quarters, insert coctail sticks, rigged with paper "sails," as masts and place on aquarium surface.*

112

Left Fruity jelly shapes, served with a bowl of fresh summer berries—an appealing combination for young and old alike. Make up some cardboard templates and cut around them, or use pastry cutters to create a variety of different shapes.

Party cakes

CREATING AN imaginative, fun cake for children can be a real challenge—as well as great fun. If you lack the time to bake a cake from scratch you need not miss out on the creative process since decorating a store-bought cake produces equally effective results. Nor do you have to spend a fortune to give a sweet treat new dimension. Simple cookies, chocolate sticks, and other children's favorites are easily transformed into creatures or characters that hold great appeal for young imaginations. So whether it's for a birthday or holiday, it is easy to design a cake that kids will love.

Right Cookies and after-dinner chocolates make up a spooky spider.

Below A sponge is transformed into a drum with icing and chocolate, sweets and lolly decorations.

Fruit

THERE ARE all sorts of ways in which fruit can be presented to children as appealing and fun. The fact that supermarkets now stock so many different and colorful tropical fruits does make life easier, as children are often drawn to their exotic appearance and sweet flavors. However, trying to give vitamin-packed citrus fruit half the appeal of the latest additive-enhanced, sugar-packed pudding pop in the shape of the latest super-hero or cartoon character can be difficult.

Younger children will be enticed by any small "mini" fruits, such as small kumquats, cherries, and grapes, along with baby apples, pears, bananas, and the more usual berries. But by being creative with more mundane fruits you will soon have youngsters of all ages digging into it with gusto. Look out for colorful fruits that add an extra decorative dimension to desserts. By adding a few balls of brightly colored melon to a simple bowl of orange slices, for example, you will immediately make the fruit look more interesting.

Making toffee apples

Scoop out apple flesh with a melon baller, place on a skewer, coat in hot caramel and allow to cool.

Below A miniature peeled pear and apple balls are coated in caramel and plunged into cold water. Form squiggles by gently pulling the toffee while malleable.

Making a mango turtle

1 *Score across the cheek of the fruit in both directions to create small squares, cutting into the flesh but taking care not to slice through the skin.*

2 *Gently push back the skin of the mango with your fingers, encouraging the scored squares to protrude and thus create a spiky effect.*

Top right A cute turtle or hedgehog is created from a cheek of mango and finished off with a fresh raspberry nose and blueberry feet.

Right A smiley face is created using standard fare from the fruit bowl, including a banana, melon, kiwi fruit, grapes, and strawberry.

Simply drinks

FROM EVERYDAY pick-me-ups such as coffee and tea to refreshing fruit juices to the occasional treat of champagne or hot winter punch, how you serve a drink can make a great difference to the way in which it is enjoyed. Attractive glassware or china will always help a drink to look more appealing, but the key is to give your imagination full reign to come up with unusual ways of quenching everyone's thirst.

Tea

T HERE ARE SO many different varieties of "tea" these days, yet some of them don't even contain a single tea leaf—they are made up of infusions of dried herbs, fruits, and other ingredients instead.

From fruit flavors such as lemon, lime, and mango, through to flowery concoctions of jasmine and rose petals, to herb infusions like chamomile, peppermint, and black currant, the choice is endless. But whatever the flavor, rules governing the making and drinking of tea are the same. It is essential to use fresh water which should be boiling when poured onto the leaves, be they dried, fresh, loose, or within bags.

Once the leaves are infused with the water, stirring will help to release their flavor. The tea should then be poured fairly quickly in order to prevent the leaves from becoming too strongly saturated and causing the infused liquid to acquire an overly strong, "stewed" taste and appearance. Whether you serve tea on its own, with milk, lemon, or iced, has to be first discussed with your guests—after all, this is one drink that seems to stir up very personal preferences!

Top left: Traditional Japanese tea is served from a simple yet elegant porcelain pot into small individual tea bowls. Fresh jasmine flowers float on the surface of each bowl, adding a fragrant flourish.

Top right: Boiling water is poured onto fresh mint leaves to make refreshing mint tea. Once steeped and poured into heat-proof glass tumblers, fresh mint sprigs add a decorative touch.

Bottom left: Iced tea is served in tall, slim glasses that have been filled with ice cubes, some containing strips of fresh lemon rind for a tangy twist.

Bottom right: Traditional English tea is poured from a warmed pot into a warmed bone china, matching cup and saucer. The leaves are strained from the infused water using a pretty silver tea strainer.

Making iced tea

1 *Remove slices of rind from a lemon with a canelli knife. Place the rind in an ice-tray, fill with water, and place in the freezer.*

2 *Make a weak pot of tea, strain and leave to cool. Pour the tea over the lemon-filled ice cubes and serve.*

Coffee

THERE IS nothing quite like a decent cup of coffee to round off a meal, be it accompanied by a brandy or liqueur or not! In fact coffee is a popular pick-me-up at any time of day—and never before has there been such a wide variety of choice. Latte, mocca, espresso, cappuccino, the long list of styles and varieties of coffee bean now available is enough to flummox even the most experienced of coffee drinkers.

The proliferation of specialized coffee bars means that you can generally buy a very good cup of coffee when you are out and about. At home, it is easy to give coffee your own special touch. Try serving coffee in unusual cups, or use a fun stencil to sprinkle chocolate or cocoa on a frothy foam-covered cappuccino. During the warmer summer months, refreshing and cooling iced café latte or chilled espresso frappé looks wonderfully appealing when served in long glasses, along with plenty of crushed or cubed ice.

Clockwise from top Filter coffee with stylish sugar twists made from waxed paper, espresso with a chocolate-dipped teaspoon; frothy cappuccino stencilled with a cocoa initia; and iced cafe latte in a tall glass.

Making iced coffee

1 *Place crushed ice in the base of a glass, then pour in strong, chilled filter or espresso coffee.*

2 *Fill the glass with a frozen milky coffee mixture that has been forked into a slushy frappé.*

Summer coolers

For a summer lunch party or a barbecue with family or friends, drinks served with an extra special twist are doubly refreshing. Fresh fruits are ideal accompaniments to summer drinks and have a particularly decorative look, especially when combined with brightly colored straws.

Homemade lemonade is a traditional summer favorite, best enjoyed well-chilled. Presented in a long glass decorated with a couple of slices of zingy lemon and lime, finished with a fun, lime-green colored straw, it is sure to provoke a thirst. Just about any long drink, from a fruit punch to a bottle of fizzy pop to sparkling mineral water, will benefit from the addition of a fruit skewer. Juicy summer berries, such as strawberries, raspberries, and blueberries, are simply threaded onto wooden skewers, interspersed with slices of kiwi fruit and cape gooseberries, and placed into individual glasses.

Left: Old-fashioned lemonade is brought up to date with a twist of lemon and lime and a citrus-green straw.

Above and left: Fruit skewers go down well with a wide range of summer drinks, especially when the berries complement the flavor of the liquid refreshment!

125

Frosted cocktails

GIVE PARTY or pre-dinner cocktails a touch of glamor and sophistication by frosting the rims of glasses and adding tiny, delicate flowers.

A simple but effective way of adding panache to a cocktail is to decorate the rim of the glass with sugar, or salt, depending on whether the ingredients are sweet or sour. The addition of a single flower provides a finishing touch.

Here, a sprig of flowering borage (*Borago officinalis*) has been used because its deep blue color complements the blue liqueur contained in the drink, and blue sugar crystals have been added to the rim-dusting to complete the effect.

Of course you can choose the flowers and sugar colorings to suit your cocktails, for example using orange or red nasturtiums (*Tropaeolum majus*) and red sugar crystals for cocktails containing reddish liqueurs. The possibilities are many, especially if you are able to gather a few flower heads from your own garden. But do make sure that any flowers you choose are nonpoisonous.

Right Pretty blue borage flowers are a subtle yet striking decoration, giving the blue-tinted cocktails an almost ethereal look . Blue sugar crystals used to frost the rim of the glass complete the sophisticated effect. Serve cocktails well chilled, with a little cubed or crushed ice— they provide the ideal refreshment for a balmy summer evening, especially when served before dinner, outside on the terrace or patio.

Adding the frosting

1 *Separate the whites of two eggs, whisk for a few seconds and pour the mixture onto a shallow plate or saucer.*

2 *Carefully dip the rim of the glass into the egg white, keeping the glass level so that the egg white covers the rim evenly.*

3 *Having sprinkled sugar and blue sugar crystals onto a flat surface, dip the glass rim into it and coat evenly with sugar.*

Winter punch

NOTHING COULD be more welcoming on a cold winter's day than a warming cup of delicious mulled wine punch, flavored with all the spices and essences associated with the season, such as orange and lemon, cinnamon, cloves, star anise, and nutmeg. Winter punch also has the advantage of looking so pretty, especially if you have the time to stud a small orange, tangerine, or kumquat with some cloves, forming a pretty and delicious decoration to float in the punch bowl.

Hot punch needs to be served with care and thought: presenting it in a decorative bowl and then ladling the liquid into small heat-proof glasses is the ideal way, although you can improvise by using a large pan or casserole dish.

However you serve the punch, do not make the mistake of allowing the mixture to boil away on the stove, as this causes all the alchohol to evaporate, so that the flavors become more concentrated and too overpowering. When making punch, it is also essential to avoid the pitfall of pouring in an assortment of wines in order to make the drink go further. This makes for an unpleasant concoction which merely wastes all the ingredients used. For optimum taste, stick to one variety of good wine.

Right: A glass bowl of mulled wine is decorated and flavored with cinnamon, fruit slices, and clove-studded tangerines.

Below: Fresh tangerines are studded with cloves to create highly fragrant decorations.

Studding tangerines

Use firm, fresh oranges, tangerines, or kumquats, and whole cloves. If the skin is tough, make holes in the fruit with a skewer before adding the cloves.

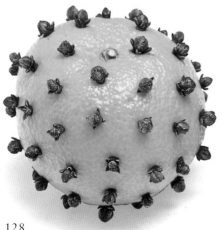

Champagne

A MUST FOR any special occasion, or even for no reason other than pure pleasure, champagne is one drink that is guaranteed to be appreciated and enjoyed. However, to enjoy champagne at its best, it needs to be treated with care. Always store bottles on their sides in a dark, cool place, and ensure the champagne is thoroughly chilled prior to serving. Try not to disturb the bottle before opening, and release the cork carefully by twisting the bottle rather than the cork itself.

I prefer to serve champagne in tall fluted glasses, as these look so elegant and also retain the bubbles for longer than the shallow style of glasses that were popular in the 1940s and '50s. Drop a fresh or frozen raspberry—either in its natural state or having been dipped into your favorite liqueur—into the bottom of the champagne flutes before pouring the bubbly to add a moment of color and style to each glass.

Left: Glass champagne flutes are assembled on a narrow black tray which has been decorated with sequin stars. A brandy-soaked raspberry at the bottom of each glass adds the final touch.

Making the glitter tray

1 *Sprinkle a generous amount of star-shaped sequins (here in shades of gold, copper, and silver) onto a dark-colored tray. Make sure you choose fairly coarse sequins, as the very fine ones have a tendency to stick to the base of the glasses.*

2 *Using the blade of a small knife, carefully maneuver the sequins into a star shape, or whatever design you choose. Make sure the flutes have dry bases before placing them on the tray to prevent the sequins from adhering to the glasses.*

Seasonal
splendor

SET YOUR TABLE according to the season with beautiful floral decorations that will dazzle your guests and provide the perfect backdrop for any type of meal. As the year progresses and different flowers and foliage come into their own, find out how to make the most of the season's natural flora and fauna to enhance any occasion. Combine these natural ingredients with tablecloths, napkins, crockery, and glassware and you will create the atmosphere you want at any time of the year.

Spring

THIS IS A time of year that seems to cry out for easy and uncluttered decorations and settings. Clean, polished, and shining glass, filled with cool water, leafy greens and natural yellows are the order of the day. Bold clusters of bright yellow daffodils and narcissi are everywhere, their trumpets heralding the arrival of longer days and better weather. Spring marks the arrival of refreshing change, along with lighter meals, new fruits, and delicate young wines.

Spring-flowering bulbs will always look wonderful on the table at this time of year, as will bunches of cut daffodils and tulips—provided that the latter are displayed in an uncontrived fashion. The less cluttered the table, the more effective it will look since the beautiful simplicity of fresh spring flowers will be totally overpowered by a rash of expensive china, flamboyant glassware, and fancy table linen that better suits the lushness of later months.

Left This fresh table has been laid for a simple, light meal. Clear and frosted glass is combined with cheerful linens in shades of green and yellow, with accents of white. Decorations within modern glass cubes are kept deliberately simple, and small, fluffy mounds of mind-your-own-business plants, set within lime-green containers, hold the candles.

Below The roots and bulbs of a flowering miniature iris are placed in a tiny aluminum pastry case tin and kept moist with some damp moss. After the meal, the bulbs may be replanted in the garden.

Summer

BALMY SUMMER evenings provide many opportunities to sit outside and enjoy a simple supper, with dusk gently descending as dessert is served. Here, delicate and fragrant lilacs and roses are arranged, with fresh green guelder rose and other interesting foliage and flowers cut from the garden, around a contemporary glass storm shade. These muted, gentle colors are ideal for summer and *al fresco* events since they have a simple, country garden air. They also lend themselves to evening entertaining, the gentle light cast by the storm-shaded candle adding a feeling of warmth. Table linen and glassware coordinate with the flowers, giving a harmonious and cohesive overall look. Even the color palette of the dessert is sympathetic to the decor, ensuring that guests' memories of the evening are enduring ones.

Left A miniature galvanized bucket makes the ideal container for an informal arrangement of garden flowers, used to decorate the table for a summer meal.

Right This delicate floral decoration has been carefully chosen to complement the linen, the glassware and even the food!

Autumn

S THE SEASON of mists and mellow fruitfulness comes upon us, a desire for informality, warmth, and cosiness takes hold. Tables draped with natural burlaps and linens, and scattered with orange and amber-colored fallen leaves, look great when laid with simple cream china, bone-handled cutlery, and simple glassware. Natural clay and terra-cotta pots and dishes also lend an earthy warmth. Baskets bound with wheat and golden corn may be filled with colored gourds, which make more of a statement than the most expensive hothouse flowers, and last twice as long. Gourds may also be used as candle holders, or to hold place cards.

Below Each guest's name is written on a traditional luggage label and secured to a gourd to mark his or her place at the table.

Right The table is laid for a harvest-time supper. Corn, wheat, gourds, tiny terra-cotta pots, and berries add autumnal color.

Winter

FLOWERS TEND to be rather expensive during the winter, but since this decoration requires a minimum of fresh materials, it is good value as well as striking. To create the table setting, a simple plastic container is thoroughly coated with metallic silver spray paint before being wrapped in a covering of silvered birch twigs. Within the container, a balled up piece of chicken-wire supports additional silvered twigs, which are arranged along with dried stems of gypsophilia, the latter's delicate and dainty heads looking much like snow flakes. Finally, freshly cut branches of winter-flowering *Viburnum tinus* and a few sprigs of evergreen foliage are added. The decoration will last for several days if well watered. Votive candles add a warming glow, while the frosted glass of the containers and a scattering of silvery glitter help to enhance the overall wintry effect.

Left A small terra-cotta pot is bound with fresh variegated ivy leaves, secured in place with a silver wire. A candle sits in the center of the pot, surrounded by fresh green "reindeer" moss.

Right Pretty snow-like heads of gypsophilia, sprigs of evergreen foliage, and silvered twigs are combined to create a striking winter tablescape. The frosty theme is reflected in the choice of a stark white tablecloth and napkins and silver and white crockery and glasses. Votive candles in frosted glass holders add a touch of warmth to the scene, causing the scattered glitter to shimmer in the flickering light.

All-year-round

THERE ARE times when guests will arrive unexpectedly, or when you are expected to throw an impromptu dinner party, and you want to make the table look especially presentable. In such cases, having an all-year-round table decoration on standby can be particularly useful. There is no need to go overboard on artificial flowers when you could put together a simple candle holder which looks very effective and can be presented alongside any fresh flowers you have available at the last moment. Alternatively, you could make use of a small flowering plant, perhaps repotting it in a pretty container for the table. Whatever the decoration, make sure that it is not so high or so prominent that it becomes a nuisance rather than an attraction on the table.

Right An old muffin tray contains votive candles set within tiny terra-cotta pots. Shiny pebbles fill some tins, and on special occasions you could use sweets or flower heads instead.

Left A small pot is covered with silk leaves, attached with double-sided tape, and used to display a flowering narcissus plant.

Parties & celebrations

WHEN PLANNING a party or a celebration, you want to make sure the occasion really goes off with a bang. Such important events can often involve weeks of planning and preparation, but they need not be hard work if you are already equipped with plenty of imaginative ideas. From weddings and anniversaries to christenings and Christmas, in this chapter you will find all the inspiration you need to guarantee that your special occasion is one that no one will ever forget.

Valentine's day

THIS IS one day when you can be as over the top as you wish, using hearts and flowers to your heart's content! Dress the table with pink and red glasses, plates, and other items and swathe it with pink or red fabrics for a romantic feel. If you prefer, you can use other flowers, such as fragrant narcissi, which look just as effective. Scatter the cloth with petals and add some evocative candlelight. Serve every course in heart-shaped molds or on heart-shaped plates. Add hearts cut from card to each napkin, scatter confetti over the underplate for each course; and tie heart-shaped cookies with ribbon and serve them with coffee.

Below Delicious petit-fours are presented on an opulent gold-rimmed plate, the theme of romance and luxury at its best!!

Right Pink champagne is served in pink flutes, with berries in red gelatin hearts on pink plates, amid red roses and candles.

Teenage party

FOR FEEDING and entertaining hoards of hungry teenagers, a barbecue is just about the most practical and sensible option. Both the decor and food can be kept very simple, using a selection of tough but attractive containers and bowls made from enamelled tin. Here, glasses are bright but inexpensive, and a blue theme is enhanced by the use of colored water-filled bottles as candle holders. The assorted bottles have been soaked in soapy water to remove their labels and the candles used are tall tapers which burn slowly and without dripping. To cater for hearty appetites, try offering a selection of at least three different "main course" foods, together with some large bowls of assorted interesting salads. Drinks should be made to look as interesting and sophisticated as possible, even if no alcohol is the rule! Choose lots of unusual shaped glasses to strike a fun note.

Below When catering for large numbers, you could make up a picnic-style box or bag for each person. Here, a small cardboard hat box has been lined with cellophane and filled with goodies, such as salads, snacks, and sandwiches.

Left Blue is the theme for this informal but sophisticated teenagers' party. Enamel platters and bowls are practical but look trendy, and bottles filled with colored water and candles make inexpensive decorations.

149

Summer lunch

A SUMMER LUNCH may not in itself be a specific celebration but it certainly provides the perfect opportunity to have a party! A long, wooden table with unfussy crystal glasses and a selection of unmatched but complementary plates based around a theme of greens provides a real *al fresco* feel, even if the weather forces you indoors. The flowers are an eclectic, seasonal melange of fragrant lilac, fluffy citrus-green alchemilla, and open roses in shades of pink. These are arranged in glass tumblers and strawberry-patterned Moroccan tea glasses (or votive holders), positioned individually along the table between place settings.

Right Summer pageants of sugar pink roses, fragrant lilacs, and fresh strawberries are arranged among an eclectic mixture of crockery in all shades of green. Check patterned napkins and chunky bone-handled cutlery add to the informality of this pretty summer party setting.

Below For the ideal summer dessert, fill a few store-bought brandy-snap baskets with creme fraîche and an assortment of summer berries. Decorate with a raspberry coulis and present on a plate with rose petals.

Kids' party bags

PARTY BAGS seem to be an obligatory aspect of any youngsters' party these days, but since store-bought bags are often overpriced and underfilled, it is far better to make your own. This also allows you to tailor the contents of each goodie bag to suit your young guests' tastes, and gives you the chance to give the bags an original theme or color scheme. Look out for colorful paper and card stock in stationery shops and give your goodie bags an individual touch by adding name tags or labels and pretty ribbons and bows

Right Pale blue and pink and candy-striped papers make colorful party bags, with labels created in minutes on a home computer.

Below Tissue paper and cellophane are shaped into bags and tied with ribbon.

Weddings

THERE ARE certain elements of a wedding celebration that people have come to expect: a beautiful bride, a gorgeous dress, a handsome groom, flowers, bridesmaids and/or page boys, champagne, speeches, and, of course, a wedding cake—usually tall, majestic-looking, and tiered. Yet there is no reason why, should you feel the urge to throw some originality into the proceedings, you cannot present some of these traditional elements in new and different ways. For example, if you are throwing a small, intimate wedding party, you might not want a grand tiered cake. So why not ring the changes by presenting miniature individual "wedding cakes" instead? Cakes for each guest are assembled on a series of glass cake stands, giving the tiered effect, but creating a far simpler and more informal feel. The cakes are easily prepared by cutting bought fruit cake into small squares, covering each square with molded icing and tying ribbon around each cake.

Right A collar of fresh flowers and foliage has been added to the base of this stylish alternative to the more traditional tiered wedding cake. The soft pinks of the flowers echo the color of the fondant, as does the small champagne flute holding a further floral posy on the top tier.

Left Rather than taking a piece of cake home wrapped in a napkin as an afterthought, this idea combines the tradition of giving wedding favors, or bon-bonnières, with wrapping the cake for guest to take home. Sugared almonds are enclosed with the wedding cake in a cellophane package, finished with ribbons.

Weddings

A WEDDING PROVIDES the perfect excuse to be as romantic as you can. A heart-shaped theme works extremely well, particularly with small canapés, and sets the tone for the rest of the proceedings.

All you need is a selection of cutters in a variety of heart-shaped sizes. Bought, sliced smoked salmon can then be cut into heart shapes with cutters and placed upon small heart-shaped biscuits and pieces of bread. Pipe the initials of the happy couple onto flat, bite-sized nibbles, or use a cut-out stencil of the letters and sprinkle a little cayenne pepper over it onto a creamy topped canapé. For a chic, minimalist look, arrange a few canapés on a large platter, along with a single well-chosen decoration, such as a fresh flower or sprig of herbs. Your guests are more likely to sample fare presented in this simple fashion than attempt to take their pick from a small plate groaning with heaps of mixed hors d'oeuvres.

Right A creamy cheese dip, served alongside savoury cheese straws, is presented in a pretty silver heart-shaped dish and decorated with a single flower.

Right Heart-shaped lollies, decorated with the bride and groom's initials, make a welcome take-home gift.

Left The clean lines of a large aluminium tray are the ideal foil for canapés including cucumber hearts topped with smoked trout pâté and caviar, and smoked salmon and piped soured cream on malted pumpernickel.

Christening

W HETHER YOU are planning a formal church service or a more informal naming ceremony, a christening is almost invariably followed by a celebratory meal. To ensure that everyone relaxes and enjoys themselves, it is usually best to opt for a cold menu, featuring as many dishes that can be prepared in advance as possible. Pink or blue flowers, depending upon whether the baby is a boy or a girl, are the usual choice of decoration. Here simple silver beakers are filled with small posies of white and blue flowers. These small posies, each of which is secured at the stem with a raffia tie, make pretty going-home gifts for friends and relatives.

Right Silver, traditional cotton and fresh spring flowers are classic choices for a christening meal. Shortbread fingers and tiny cucumber sandwiches are always popular, especially when washed down with cold champagne.

Below Blue and white flowers make up fragrant place setting decorations. Secured with a rubber band, the posies are kept in water until required, when the stems are dried and the band concealed with blue ribbon.

Golden oldies

A GOLDEN WEDDING celebration is a great occasion, especially in this day and age, when it is seen as something of an achievement, too! A gold and yellow color scheme is appropriate as well as classic, and will be especially appreciated by an older age group. This gilded pear centerpiece is rather extravagant since it incorporates a large amount of gold and gold leaf, but it certainly makes an impression! You can find gold leaf in any good craft shop, and it is ideal for covering fruits, berries, leaves, and flowers.

The gold and yellow theme is carried through in the use of plates, bowls, and glasses decorated with gold motifs. Chocolates wrapped in gilded papers and foils will look wonderful scattered upon the table, perhaps with sequins or other sparkling ornaments, while cords and ribbons add a pretty flourish to napkins and menu cards. Plenty of petals and flowers add an essential finishing touch.

Right Stems of yellow roses and gilded pears are wired together in a pyramid shape before being placed on an elegant cake stand. Crumpled gold leaf is added between the gaps to create a stunning centerpiece.

Gilding pears

1 *Ensure that the pear is clean and dry and then use gold spray to give a light, even covering.*

2 *Cover the pear with a sheet of gold leaf and use a paintbrush to attach it to the skin of the fruit.*

Christmas

A PRETTY JAR or bottle of homemade preserved fruits or spiced pickles ...es an ideal Christmas gift. These may ...repared well in advance during the ...nn when fruits such as plums, pears, ...nes, and apricots are more plentiful ...nexpensive. Spiced fruits also provide ...come change from everyday chutneys ...ickles when offered alongside sliced ...neats. If you do not have the time to ...re spiced fruits yourself, you can ...s buy them from the supermarket ...mply repackage them in jars of your ...along with some fresh bay leaves and ...lful of cloves.

Left Unusual glass jars are used to hold spiced pears, fruit conserve, and bottled flavored oils.

Below Mini English Christmas puddings, made within traditional cloth pudding bags, also make lovely gifts.

Left: White royal icing is piped onto gingerbread shapes, made with cookie cutters and paper templates. If you don't have time to make your own, simply add icing to store-bought ones.

Right: A wooden bowl is filled with nuts, some decorated with edible gold paint, filigree baubles, and iced cookies. The tree is draped with strings of threaded fresh cranberries.

Christmas

CHRISTMAS IS one time of year when almost everyone will entertain and will make an extra effort both in decorating the home and in what they serve to their guests in the way of food and drink. Unfortunately, there just never seems to be enough time to prepare for the festivities, which is why it seems sensible to utilise as many shop-bought foods and decorative elements as possible, most of which require little extra enhancement.

Even a simple bowl of fruit or nuts can be transformed into a stunning table centre with little effort, by using edible gold and silver paints, jewel-like cranberries and a few well chosen baubles. Add a few prettily iced biscuits, tied up with ribbons, and you have a host of decorations that are good enough to eat!

Christmas

ICE BOWLS always look spectacular and yet they are so simple to make: all you need are the right sized bowls and a little storage space in the deep freeze! For Christmas, fresh cranberries and a colored sequins add a seasonal sparkle, although you can create more natural versions using spices such as star anise, cloves, and cinnamon, and citrus fruit slices, which look equally festive. Ice bowls will last for some time, and can be used to serve icecreams and sorbets, or even chocolates and petits-fours at the conclusion of a meal. They also look magical when filled with a mixture of berries and fruits, especially if you also make a smaller version and use that to serve cream or ice cream at the same time.

Making an ice bowl

1 *Secure a small freezer-proof bowl inside a larger one with tape, leaving a 1 in gap. Fill the gap with berries, sequins, and glitter, then pour in filtered or bottled water.*

2 *Leave for several hours until frozen solid. Place bowls in a few inches of hot water to loosen them, then remove the ice bowl and store in the freezer until required.*

Right This glamorous ice bowl has been filled with ice cream and topped with fresh cranberries. It would be ideal for serving fresh fruit salad or sorbets. Although the ice will eventually melt, the bowl will certainly last for at least a couple of hours.

Above Star-shaped icing sugar motifs, sifted through a tea strainer, cheer up store-bought pies. Use a cookie cutter as the template, draw around it in pencil and then cut it out with a scissors or a craft knife.

Easter

When Easter comes around, and with it the promise of warmer weather and longer days, we can look forward to enjoying the fresh flavors and colors of spring. Tasty spring lamb, crisp root vegetables, and miniature new potatoes are available in abundance, and newly blooming plants and flowers provide plenty of inspiration for Easter decorations.

Invigorating spring greens and cheerful yellows are always a good starting point, while pastel shades, such as duck egg blues and pale pinks, and creams can all evoke a feeling of spring-like freshness.

When deciding on your menu, try to opt for fresh and light flavors and include as many locally grown and produced items as possible. Salad ingredients begin to improve dramatically at this time of year, and the first crops of tiny new potatoes are delicious when served hot or used in a salad.

Right Mint sauce and steamed spring vegetables accompany a rosemary and garlic-studded saddle of lamb. A simple bowl of fragrant narcissi, hyacinths, and ranunculus add the final flourish.

Above Hard-boiled eggs, painted in pastel shades with water-based nontoxic paints and dotted with speckles using a non-.toxic black pen, make great decorations for the Easter table.

Left A salad of warm new potatoes and soft-boiled quail's eggs, several of which are served within their beautiful mottled and speckled shells.

Easter

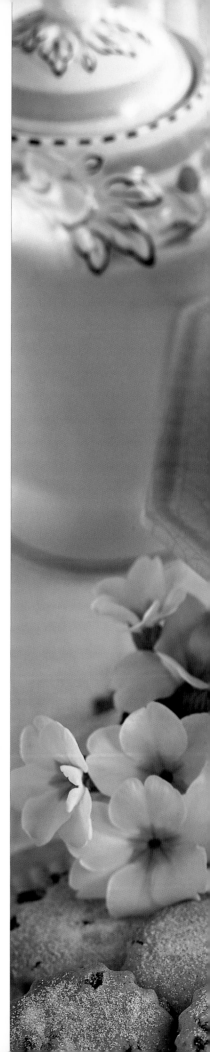

A<small>N EASTER-THEMED</small> afternoon tea is a good way of entertaining family and friends over the holiday without having to go to the trouble and expense of serving up a cooked meal. In England, an integral part of this Easter celebration is a "simnel cake," a kind of rich fruitcake with a traditional topping of buttery yellow marzipan. To continue the pretty yellow theme, fresh common primroses are used to decorate the cake and the table, giving it a fresh, spring-like feel. Round off the spread with simple sandwiches and currant-studded spiced Easter buns, and then all you have to do is to provide plenty of freshly brewed tea!

Right English simnel cake is traditionally decorated with a layer of marzipan, which is topped by eleven marzipan balls to represent the eleven apostles, without Judas.

Below Scrambled eggs are extremely simple to make and a practical way to serve eggs to several people. For an appropriate Easter flourish, serve them in a cleaned egg shell.

ACKNOWLEDGMENTS

A LITANY OF THANKS to the following people, without whom this book would not be what and where it is today:

To *Susan Berry,* my commissioning editor and by now, brilliant, patient, and wise friend, a million thanks for creating the team who worked on this title, for the help throughout and for keeping us all going.

To *Mandy Lebentz* for her careful and attentive editing of my rambling, but almost always promptly delivered, text. To *Carole Handslip*, the calm and unflappable home economist whose experienced hands were able to transform my paper dreams into edible reality. To *Amanda Heywood*, ably assisted by *Vanessa Kellas,* for recording my dreams and Carole's handiwork into a feast of photographs and for her incredible styling prowess. Thank you also to all the work on the design front by *Debbie Mole.*

I must also express my sincere thanks to *Jonny Atkinson, Ruth Harris, Jaynie Heynes, Jill Roach,* and *Jon Poulsom* for keeping the flower side of my life on top form while I have been sojourning in the world of food.

Lastly my thanks are for *Nicholas* who, with his characteristic acceptance, has tolerated life being rather free from flourishes recently and for whom my love continues to flourish.